PENGUIN BOOKS

Wobble

Wobble

35 Tantalising Jellies

Rachael Lane

Contents

Jellies

Introduction

Jelly was once a decadent sign of great opulence, gracing the banquet tables of the rich and royal in medieval times. Today, sadly, this versatile dish is thought of by many as a mere childhood confection made out of sugary crystals from a brightly-coloured box. However, jelly is a truly unique and enticing food. Visually impressive and highly sophisticated, with that tantalising wobble that cannot help but evoke a sense of fun and childhood nostalgia, jelly is gently jiggling its way back onto our tables and into our hearts and imaginations.

Gelatine was discovered in England in the 14th Century. Its lengthy preparation meant jellies were a luxury afforded by only the very wealthy. However, over time, gelatine became more accessible to the general public and was first commercially produced in its dry granule form in the mid 1800s. In the early 1900s, these granules were coloured and flavoured, and sold in the crystal form that many recognise as jelly today.

Jelly is so much more than a just-add-water-and-set, artificially coloured and flavoured dessert. Almost any kind of liquid can be turned into a jelly, and almost any vessel can be used as a mould – so the possibilities for extraordinary flavours and dramatic shapes are endless. This book is full of remarkable recipes, from child-friendly fruit jellies to more elegant and complex jellies infused with alcohol, herbs, spices or nuts.

Basic jelly-making is very simple, requiring only a few readily-available everyday pieces of kitchen equipment. The more advanced techniques, such as layering, suspending and bombes, require a little more time and patience, but are well worth the effort for their stunning visual impact. Follow the recipes in this book carefully if you are just starting out with jelly-making, and when you are confident of your skills, use the information on the following pages to help you create your own unique shapes and flavours.

Jelly appeals to the child, the gourmand and the mad scientist in all of us – its infamous wobble is sure to bring a smile or mischievous giggle to children and adults alike.

EQUIPMENT

Fine-mesh sieve Used to strain jelly mixtures and fruit to remove all impurities for a clear and transparent jelly. Often lined with a double layer of muslin cloth.

Heatproof bowls Most often made from ceramic or tempered glass (such as Pyrex), heatproof bowls are needed for placing over a saucepan of simmering water when gently dissolving softened gelatine in liquid.

Measuring jugs Used to measure liquid, essential for calculating how much gelatine is required.

Moulds Jelly moulds can range from simple to ornate. Moulds come in many shapes and sizes and can be made from a variety of materials – from modern plastic, silicone or metal moulds, to older varieties made from glass or ceramic, as well as antique copper moulds. Just about anything can be used as a jelly mould, as long as it's water-tight and, if metal, non-reactive. Cake pans, bowls, cups and glasses all work well if you can't get your hands on custom-made jelly moulds. However, metal and plastic moulds are easier to use than glass or ceramic ones, as glass and ceramic are poor conductors of heat, making it more difficult to quickly warm and unmould jellies. Avoid using anything with a varying thickness (such as a glass with a very heavy base) as it will take longer for the thick parts of the mould to warm up when unmoulding. If using antique copper moulds, ensure they are tin-lined.

Muslin cloth A tightly-woven cotton fabric, used for straining in jelly-making for two purposes. Firstly, it is used to strain cooked or puréed fruits, in order to extract a clear juice from the pulp. Secondly, it is used to strain the jelly mixture after the gelatine has been dissolved, to remove any undissolved particles of gelatine, ensuring a smooth jelly. Muslin cloth can be purchased from speciality food-supply stores and fabric shops. It is inexpensive and can be washed and re-used many times. Always wash before first use.

SETTING AGENTS

Gelatine

Gelatine is a setting agent made from animal-derived collagen. It can be used to set a variety of both sweet and savoury liquids into a solid form with that distinctive and beloved wobble. Gelatine-set jelly will slowly melt when at room temperature, so must be kept chilled and served reasonably quickly once removed from the refrigerator, especially on a hot day. The addition of extra gelatine can stabilise a jelly at room temperature for longer periods. The low melting temperature gives jelly its pleasing melt-in-the-mouth quality.

Gelatine can be found in two forms, leaf and powdered, and in different setting strengths, also known as 'blooms'. Leaf gelatine is most readily available in titanium strength and gold strength, whereas powdered gelatine is most commonly gold strength. It is essential to know the strength of your gelatine to ensure successful setting. This can be a little tricky, as the strength is not always marked on the packaging and, even if it is, there is no standardisation for strength between brands. Therefore, one brand of titanium-strength gelatine can differ in setting strength to another, making it difficult to easily substitute brands. While this may sound daunting, the following pages contain some simple tests you can carry out and other hints and tips to help you make perfectly wobbly jelly every time.

Testing setting strength

The gelatine strength and quantities used in the recipes in this book, and in the conversion chart on page 5, refer to Gelita brand leaf gelatine and Davis brand powdered gelatine. If you are using a different brand of gelatine, ascertain the strength by doing a test setting, using 1 cup (250 ml/8 ½ fl oz) of prepared cordial.

- If your brand's strength is labelled, test using the same quantities recommended in the conversion chart on page 5.

- If you are using unlabelled leaf gelatine, weigh a single leaf of gelatine using digital scales.

WEIGHT	TEST
4 g (0.14 oz)	test as per titanium strength
2 g (0.07 oz)	test as per gold strength

- If you are using unlabelled powdered gelatine. test using the quantities recommended in the conversion chart on page 5.

After testing, adjust the quantity of gelatine if necessary to achieve the level of setness you require. Use your findings along with the conversion chart on page 5 to determine the quantity of gelatine needed for your chosen recipe.

Leaf gelatine

Gelatine leaves are transparent, rectangular sheets of dried gelatine. They come in a range of strengths, but most commonly in titanium and gold. Leaf gelatine can be found in packets of 6–12 at speciality food-supply stores or select gourmet delicatessens.

Titanium strength gelatine is industrial strength and is the highest quality leaf gelatine available, about double the strength of gold-strength gelatine. The sheets are thicker than the gold strength and produce a clearer set jelly.

Gold strength gelatine is commercial strength and is the most readily available leaf gelatine. It can be substituted easily with powdered gelatine:

1 leaf gold-strength gelatine = 1 teaspoon powdered gelatine.

However, this can differ from brand to brand. Always set a test jelly (see page 3) if using brands of gelatine not used in this book.

Powdered gelatine

Powdered gelatine is available from supermarkets. When set, jellies made with powdered gelatine are often a little cloudy and have a slight aftertaste. It is therefore not the superior choice for jelly-making. Powdered gelatine is better suited to the more full-flavoured, vibrant coloured jellies, and not a good choice for any transparent jellies with subtle flavours.

Blooming gelatine

Softening gelatine, or blooming, as it is also known, is a vital step in jelly-making. The gelatine is soaked in cold water to rehydrate and soften in preparation for dissolving, to help achieve a smooth texture in your finished jelly. Softening, or blooming, is necessary for both leaf and powdered gelatine.

To soften leaf gelatine – fully immerse in cold liquid and leave to soak for 5–10 minutes to rehydrate and soften. This can take slightly longer when using milk. When gelatine is being added to a hot jelly base, soak in a separate bowl of cold water, and, once softened, drain and squeeze out any excess moisture from the gelatine before stirring into the hot jelly base. When gelatine is being added to a cold jelly base, place in a heatproof bowl and add enough of the cold jelly base to cover. Once softened, set the bowl over a saucepan of simmering water and heat gently, until dissolved. Remove from the heat and add the remaining cold jelly base (always add the cold liquid to the warm gelatine mixture, and not the other way around, otherwise the gelatine can set in lumps).

To soften powdered gelatine – pour a small amount of the jelly base into a bowl and sprinkle the powdered gelatine over the surface. Leave to soak for 5–10 minutes to rehydrate and soften. Stir into a hot jelly base or, if adding to a cold base, heat gently over a saucepan of simmering water, until dissolved.

Agar agar

Agar agar is a setting agent derived from seaweed, and is a vegetarian substitute for gelatine. It is commonly used in many Asian countries for making fruit- and coconut-based jellies, and can be found in health-food shops and Asian food stores. Agar agar is much sturdier and more stable than gelatine as it has a high melting temperature. To dissolve, it needs to be added to boiling liquid and it sets quickly without requiring refrigeration. Agar agar jellies can be kept at room temperature and will not begin to melt until brought back towards boiling point.

Unfortunately, the stability and high melting temperature of agar agar results in a jelly that lacks the melt-in-the-mouth quality and the wobbliness of gelatine-set jellies. However, the advantages, besides being great for vegetarians, are that agar agar jelly does not need to be refrigerated – so it's great for outdoor parties or picnics – and its firmness means it can be easily sliced into cubes or cut into shapes with a cookie-cutter.

Agar agar is best used for strong-tasting fruit-, milk- or cream-based jellies, as it remains cloudy and has a slight aftertaste when set.

CONVERSION CHART

Soft set jelly is firm but still springy when gently touched. For jelly that is served in the mould.
Firm set jelly is firm when gently touched. For jelly that is to be unmoulded.

	GELITA TITANIUM-STRENGTH LEAF GELATINE	GELITA GOLD-STRENGTH LEAF GELATINE	DAVIS POWDERED GELATINE	LOTUS AGAR AGAR POWDER
Soft set	1 leaf	2 leaves	2 teaspoons	¼ teaspoon
Firm set	1½ leaves	3 leaves	3 teaspoons	½ teaspoon
Milk soft set	½ leaf	1½ leaves	1½ teaspoons	¼ teaspoon
Milk firm set	1 leaf	2 leaf	2 teaspoons	½ teaspoon

All measures are for 1 cup (250 ml/8½ fl oz) liquid.

SUGAR SYRUP

Sugar syrup is used to adjust the sweetness of fruit-based jelly mixtures. Fruit sweetness varies according to variety, ripeness and seasonality. The amount of added sweetness required can therefore differ with every batch of fruit. Use the suggested measure in the recipe as a guide and add sugar syrup to taste. Make your mixture a little sweeter than you like, as flavour and sweetness diminishes when food is chilled.

Sugar syrup can be made in small batches, as required, or make larger quantities and store in the refrigerator for up to two weeks.

Sugar Syrup

MAKES 2 CUPS (500 ML/17 FL OZ)

- 1 cup (220 g/8 oz) sugar
- 1 cup (250 ml/8½ fl oz) water

1   Combine the sugar and water in a small saucepan and stir occasionally over low heat until the sugar dissolves. Remove from the heat and set aside to cool.

2   Use immediately, or store in an airtight container in the refrigerator for up to two weeks.

HINTS & TIPS

Before you start

Most of the jellies in this book are suitable to be made as a single large jelly or as smaller individual jellies. If making multiple jellies, divide the mixture evenly between the moulds. Measure the capacity of your mould or moulds by filling with water then emptying into a measuring jug. You may need to adjust the recipe quantities to suit the mould capacity.

Factors that affect setting

- Acid and alcohol Citric acid in fruit such as lemons, oranges and limes, and high proof alcohol can weaken the setting-strength of gelatine. Do not use alcohol 45 per cent proof or higher, as it will prevent the gelatine from setting.

- Boiling Do not boil gelatine as it weakens its setting properties.

- Milk Also know as blancmange, jellies made with milk set firmer than those made from other liquids and therefore require less gelatine.

- Protein-destroying enzymes Tropical fruits such as pineapple, kiwifruit, and mango, as well as figs and ginger, contain enzymes which break down the protein in gelatine and prevent it from setting. Cook these fruits before use, or use canned fruits or juice, as heat destroys the enzyme.

Continued

- **Refrigeration** The longer a jelly is refrigerated the firmer it sets.

- **Freezing** Do not freeze jelly as it destroys the gelatine. When defrosted it will be a runny mess.

Time savers

- Store-bought juices or syrups can be used instead of fresh fruit when making jelly. Juices such as blueberry, cherry, cranberry, clear apple and orange, as well as tinned pineapple juice, are ideal for making jelly.

- Speed up the setting process by quickly cooling your jelly mixture over a bowl of iced water. Stir constantly, until it begins to thicken but not set. Pour into the mould immediately and refrigerate.

Clarity

- Always strain cooked or puréed fruit through a muslin-lined sieve to extract a clear, vibrant juice. Do not squeeze, press or vigorously stir fruit pulp such as tomato, rhubarb or strawberry, as this will make the strained juice cloudy.

- Strain jelly mixture through a muslin-lined sieve after the gelatine has been added and dissolved, to remove undissolved gelatine particles. Thick mixtures, such as jelly containing mango pulp, and blancmange mixtures with added ricotta, mascarpone or goat's cheese should be passed through a fine-mesh sieve to remove any lumps.

Serving

- If serving jelly shots in glasses, take them out of the refrigerator for 5–10 minutes, to allow them to come to room temperature. Briefly dip the base of the shot glass in boiling water to help them to release easily from the glass.

- Serve alcohol-based jellies responsibly. Alcohol takes longer to digest when consumed as jelly, so the effects can sneak up on even the most experienced drinkers. Be sure to inform your guests.

- To cut jelly, always use a heated, thin-bladed knife. This will ensure a clean slice and prevent tearing.

Storage

Store gelatine, both leaf and powdered, in an airtight container kept in a cool, dry, odourless place. This is particularly necessary if you live in a damp or humid climate.

JELLY TECHNIQUES

Unmoulding

1 Fill a sink with hot water, dip the jelly mould in (be careful not to get any water inside the mould) and hold for a few seconds. This melts the outside of the jelly, so do not do this for any longer than necessary. Immersion time will vary

depending on the mould you have used. Metal and plastic moulds heat quickly and only require 2–5 seconds. Ceramic, glass and silicon moulds can take 10–30 seconds, or longer, depending on the thickness and insulating properties of the mould.

2 Use your fingertips to gently pull the jelly away from the sides of the mould to release the vacuum.

3 Lightly wet the plate you are using for unmoulding (this will allow the jelly to be moved after it is unmoulded). Place the plate face-down over the mould and, firmly holding the plate and mould together, quickly invert. You will hear a 'slurp' sound as the jelly comes away from the mould. You may need to coax the jelly out by repeating step two, or by sharply shaking the mould whilst inverted. If the jelly still does not release easily, repeat step one.

Layering

Semi-set stage When creating layered jelly, it is essential that each layer is semi set before adding the liquid for the next layer. This ensures the base layer is set enough to stop it from merging with the new layer, yet tacky enough for the new layer to adhere. If the jelly is too firmly set, the layers will separate when unmoulded. Setting time will depend on the thickness of the layer and the size of the mould.

Pouring When adding layers, pour the mixture slowly over the back of a dessert spoon set against the inside of the mould, to allow the mixture to gently cover the base layer without disturbing it.

Reheating jelly mixture When creating a jelly with multiple layers, your jelly mixture may start to set before you are ready to use it. If this happens, simply set the bowl containing the mixture over a saucepan of simmering water and heat gently, stirring until smooth. Remember to ensure it has cooled sufficiently before use, or else it will melt the layer below. Jelly mixtures can be reheated in this way several times before their setting ability starts to weaken.

Agar agar When using agar agar, you need to work quickly, as it sets much faster than gelatine. Before adding a layer, lightly scratch the surface of the jelly with the tines of a fork to help the layers to adhere. Jelly set with agar agar can withstand the addition of a warm mixture as it has a higher melting temperature than gelatine-set jelly.

Bombes

Bombes are created when two or more layers of jelly are set inside of each other. Cutting into a bombe jelly reveals its hidden centre.

Moulds You need two similar-shaped moulds or bowls, one at least 25 per cent smaller than the other. The smaller mould needs to fit inside the larger one, leaving enough space to create a substantial jelly layer between the two.

Calculating quantities If your moulds are a different capacity to the ones recommended in the recipe you will need to calculate new quantities to adjust the recipe.

· Fill each mould with water and then pour into a measuring jug.

Continued

9

- Subtract the capacity of the smaller mould from the capacity of the outer mould and you have the quantity of mixture that you require to make the outer layer of the bombe. Make just a little extra, in case of any spills.

Creating the Bombe

1 Place the larger mould on a tray and pour in the jelly mixture for the outer layer.

2 Set the smaller mould on top and fill with pie weights, dried beans or rice, until it is weighed down enough to make the outer jelly mixture rise up to fill the space between the two moulds.

3 Making sure the inner mould is centred, secure with two strips of sticky tape across the top of the moulds. Top up the outer layer with additional mixture, if required. Refrigerate until firmly set.

4 Remove the tape and discard the weights. Half-fill the inner mould with hot water and leave for 10–15 seconds, to slightly melt the surface of the jelly below. Place your fingers inside the inner mould and gently twist and lift, until the mould is released. Refrigerate until the softened jelly re-sets.

5 Pour in the jelly mixture for the inner layer so it is flush with the top of the outer layer (or you can fill higher so that it covers the top of the outer layer which will give you a jelly with a different-coloured base). Refrigerate until firmly set before unmoulding.

Suspending

Fruit, edible flowers, nuts and even gold leaf can be suspended and set inside jelly. Suspension can be achieved in two ways.

Layering A layer of clear jelly is first semi set in the bottom of the mould. Arrange your items on the jelly and cover carefully with another layer of jelly mixture. Repeat this process as many times as you wish.

Dispersion Place the jelly mixture over a bowl of iced water and stir continuously until it cools and begins to thicken. Add your items and gently stir through the mixture to disperse. Pour immediately into the mould. The items should suspend in the thickened jelly mixture, rather than sinking to the bottom. Be mindful not to allow the jelly mixture to over set before adding the items, otherwise you will create air bubbles when stirring, which will set inside your jelly.

Stained glass

A stained-glass jelly is created by suspending cubes of two or more different-coloured jellies in a contrasting-coloured jelly or blancmange. Suspension can be achieved using either the layering or dispersion techniques, depending on the desired effect. Serve in slices to reveal the stained glass effect.

Quince & Orange Blossom

- 1½ cups (330 g/11½ oz) sugar
- juice of ½ lemon
- 3 quinces, peeled, cored and cut into quarters
- ½ teaspoon orange-blossom water
- 6 leaves gold-strength gelatine, cut into quarters

MOULD

any – total capacity of 2 cups (500 ml/17 fl oz)

To save time, you can cook the quinces in a pressure cooker on the lowest setting for 45 minutes. Keep leftover poaching syrup to sweeten yoghurt, or to poach or stew other fruits such as plums or pears.

1   Preheat an oven to 150°C (300°F).

2   Combine the sugar and lemon juice with 1½ cups (375 ml/12½ fl oz) water in an ovenproof saucepan over low heat, stirring occasionally, until the sugar dissolves. Remove from the heat and add the quince. Cover and cook in the oven for 4–5 hours, until quince is pink and tender.

3   Transfer the quince and ½ cup (125 ml/4 fl oz) of the poaching liquid to a medium-sized bowl. Mash together using a potato masher, then spoon into a muslin-lined sieve and set aside to strain for about 15 minutes. Occasionally stir gently, but do not scrape or press the mixture through the cloth as this will make the juice cloudy.

4   Pour the juice into a measuring jug. Add the orange-blossom water and enough water to make 2 cups (500 ml/17 fl oz) in total.

5   Place the gelatine in a medium-sized heatproof bowl and pour in just enough quince mixture to cover. Set aside for 5–10 minutes, until the gelatine has softened.

6   Set the bowl over a saucepan of simmering water and heat gently, stirring occasionally, until the gelatine dissolves. Remove from the heat, add the remaining quince mixture and stir to combine.

7   Strain through a muslin-lined sieve and into the mould. Skim off any bubbles and refrigerate for 2–4 hours, until firm set.

8   Unmould to serve.

SERVES 4

Strawberries and Cream

- strawberry slices, to decorate

STRAWBERRY JELLY

- 500 g (1 lb 2 oz) strawberries, hulled and coarsely chopped
- ¼ cup (55 g/2 oz) caster sugar
- juice of ½ lemon
- ½ cup (125 ml/4 fl oz) sugar syrup (page 7)
- 1 teaspoon rosewater
- 6 leaves gold-strength gelatine, cut into quarters

VANILLA BLANCMANGE

- 1 cup (250 ml/8½ fl oz) full-cream milk
- 1 tablespoon (15 g/½ oz) sugar
- ½ vanilla bean, split lengthways
- 2 leaves gold-strength gelatine, cut into quarters

MOULD

any – total capacity of 3 cups (750 ml/25 fl oz)

1 To prepare the strawberry jelly, place the strawberries, sugar and lemon juice in a medium-sized bowl and mash together using a potato masher. Set aside for 30 minutes.

2 Pour the strawberry mixture into a muslin-lined sieve and set aside to strain for about 30 minutes. Occasionally stir gently, but do not scrape or press the mixture through the cloth as this will make the juice cloudy.

3 To prepare the vanilla blancmange, combine the milk, sugar and vanilla bean in a small saucepan over low heat, stirring occasionally for 3–5 minutes or until it begins to simmer. Remove from the heat and set aside for 15 minutes, to infuse and cool.

4 Pour the strained strawberry juice into a measuring jug. Add the sugar syrup, rosewater and enough water to make 2 cups (500 ml/17 fl oz) in total. Set aside to cool.

5 Place the gelatine for both jellies in separate medium-sized heatproof bowls and pour in just enough of the liquids to cover. Set aside for 5–10 minutes, until the gelatine has softened.

6 Set each bowl over a saucepan of simmering water and heat gently, stirring occasionally, until the gelatine dissolves. Remove from the heat, add the remainder of each liquid and stir to combine.

CONTINUED

7 Strain the liquids separately through a muslin-lined sieve (rinse the cloth between each batch). Cover the vanilla blancmange mixture and keep at room temperature until required.

8 Arrange the strawberry slices in the base of the mould. Pour in ½ cup (125 ml/4 fl oz) of the strawberry mixture and skim off any bubbles. Refrigerate for 10–30 minutes, until semi set.

9 Add another ½ cup (125 ml/4 fl oz) of strawberry mixture, pouring slowly over the back of a dessert spoon resting against the inside of the mould. Refrigerate for 10–30 minutes, until semi set.

10 Add the vanilla blancmange, pouring over the back of a spoon as before, and refrigerate for 10–30 minutes, until semi set.

11 Pour in the remaining strawberry mixture and refrigerate for 2–3 hours, until firm set.

12 Unmould to serve.

SERVES 6

Leftover strawberry pulp can be frozen, or refrigerated and used within 3 days, to make sorbet, muffins or cakes.

Apple and Rhubarb

RHUBARB JELLY
- 500 g (1 lb 2 oz) rhubarb, cut into 5 cm (2 in) lengths
- ¾ cup (170 g/6 oz) sugar
- 1½ leaves titanium-strength gelatine, cut into quarters

APPLE JELLY
- 1 cup (250 ml/8½ fl oz) clear apple juice
- 3 tablespoons (60 ml/2 fl oz) sugar syrup (page 7)
- 1½ leaves titanium-strength gelatine, cut into quarters

MOULD
any – total capacity of 4 cups (1 L/34 fl oz)

1   To prepare the rhubarb jelly, combine the rhubarb and sugar with ¾ cup (180 ml/6 fl oz) water in a medium-sized saucepan. Stew the rhubarb over low heat for 10–15 minutes, until the rhubarb is soft and has lost its shape.

2   Pour the stewed rhubarb into a muslin-lined sieve and set aside to strain for about 15 minutes. Occasionally stir gently, but do not scrape or press the mixture through the cloth as this will make the juice cloudy.

3   Pour the strained rhubarb juice into a measuring jug. Add enough water to make 1½ cups (375 ml/12½ fl oz) in total. Set aside to cool.

4   Meanwhile, to prepare the apple jelly, combine the apple juice and sugar syrup with 3 tablespoons (60 ml/2 fl oz) water in a bowl.

5   Place the gelatine for both jellies in separate medium-sized heatproof bowls and pour in just enough of the liquids to cover. Set aside for 5–10 minutes, until the gelatine has softened.

6   Set each bowl over a saucepan of simmering water and heat gently, stirring occasionally, until the gelatine dissolves. Remove from the heat, add the remainder of each liquid and stir to combine.

7   Strain the liquids separately through a muslin-lined sieve (rinse the cloth between each batch). Cover the apple mixture and keep at room temperature until required.

CONTINUED

8 Pour the rhubarb mixture into the mould and skim off any bubbles. Refrigerate for 1½ hours, until semi set.

9 Add the apple mixture, pouring slowly over the back of a dessert spoon resting against the inside of the mould.

10 Refrigerate for 4–5 hours, until firm set.

11 Unmould to serve.

SERVES 4

Rhubarb pulp can be frozen, or refrigerated and used within 3 days. Place a dollop on top of your muesli, or serve with yoghurt for breakfast or a quick snack.

Tropical Layer

MANGO JELLY
- 250 g (9 oz) mango flesh
- 1½ tablespoons (30 ml/1 fl oz) sugar syrup (page 7)
- 1½ leaves gold-strength gelatine, cut into quarters

PINEAPPLE JELLY
- 100 ml (3½ fl oz) tinned pineapple juice
- 1½ tablespoons (30 ml/1½ fl oz) sugar syrup (page 7)
- 1½ leaves gold-strength gelatine, cut into quarters

PASSIONFRUIT JELLY
- 100 ml (3½ fl oz) passionfruit juice
- 1½ tablespoons (30 ml/1½ fl oz) sugar syrup (page 7)
- 1½ leaves gold-strength gelatine, cut into quarters

COCONUT JELLY
- 100 ml (3½ fl oz) coconut milk
- 1½ tablespoons (30 ml/1½ fl oz) sugar syrup (page 7)
- 1 leaf gold-strength gelatine, cut into quarters

MOULD
any – total capacity of 2 cups (500 ml/17 fl oz)

1 To prepare the mango jelly, coarsely chop the mango and combine with 1 cup (250 ml/8½ fl oz) water in a small saucepan. Cook over low–medium heat for 5–10 minutes, until softened and cooked through. Transfer to a small food-processor and blend until smooth, or mash with a potato masher. Stir in the sugar syrup and strain through a fine-mesh sieve into a medium-sized heatproof bowl. Set aside to cool.

2 Combine the liquid ingredients for each of the remaining jellies in separate medium-sized heatproof bowls. Add the gelatine to each of the bowls, including the mango mixture. Set aside for 5–10 minutes, until the gelatine has softened.

3 Set each bowl over a saucepan of simmering water and heat gently, stirring occasionally, until the gelatine dissolves.

4 Strain the liquids separately through a muslin-lined sieve (rinse the cloth between each batch). Cover the pineapple, passionfruit and coconut mixtures and keep at room temperature until required.

5 Pour half the mango mixture into the base of the mould and skim off any bubbles. Refrigerate for 10 minutes, until semi set.

6 Pour in one third of the coconut mixture, pouring the mixture slowly over the back of a dessert spoon resting against the inside of the mould, and refrigerate for 5–10 minutes, until semi set.

7 Create another two layers using the pineapple and passionfruit mixtures, followed by a second coconut layer, pouring and setting as before. Continue in this fashion with the remaining mixtures. Refrigerate for 2 hours, or until firm set.

8 Unmould to serve.

SERVES 4

Watermelon and Mint

- 2 tablespoons (30 g/1 oz) sugar
- 6 sprigs fresh mint, plus extra for garnish (optional)
- 500 g (1 lb 2 oz) seedless watermelon, coarsely chopped
- 3 leaves titanium-strength gelatine, cut into quarters

MOULD
any – total capacity of 3 cups (750 ml/25 fl oz)

1 Combine the sugar with ½ cup (125 ml/4 fl oz) water in a small saucepan. Simmer over low heat for 2–3 minutes, stirring occasionally, until the sugar dissolves. Add the mint and simmer for 2 minutes. Remove from the heat and set aside for 10 minutes, to infuse.

2 Meanwhile, place the watermelon in a food processor and blend until smooth. Pour into a muslin-lined sieve and set aside to strain for 5–10 minutes.

3 Place the gelatine in a medium-sized heatproof bowl and pour in just enough strained watermelon juice to cover. Set aside for 5–10 minutes, until the gelatine has softened.

4 Set the bowl over a saucepan of simmering water and heat gently, stirring occasionally, until the gelatine dissolves. Remove from the heat, add the remaining watermelon juice and the mint-infused syrup, and stir to combine.

5 Strain the liquid through a muslin-lined sieve into a measuring jug. If necessary, add enough water to make 2 cups (500 ml/17 fl oz) in total.

6 Pour into the mould and refrigerate for 2 hours, or until firm set.

7 Unmould and garnish with mint leaves (if using) to serve.

SERVES 4–6

Lemon Verbena and Mint Bombe

LEMON VERBENA JELLY
- ½ cup (125 ml/4 fl oz) sugar syrup (page 7)
- 2 tablespoons (40 ml/1½ fl oz) freshly squeezed lemon juice
- 40 fresh lemon verbena leaves
- 1¾ leaves titanium-strength gelatine, cut into quarters

LEMON VERBENA & MINT BLANCMANGE
- 1¼ cup (310 ml/10½ fl oz) full-cream milk
- ½ cup (125 ml/4 fl oz) sugar syrup (page 7)
- 20 fresh lemon verbena leaves
- 20 fresh mint leaves
- 1¼ leaves titanium-strength gelatine, cut into quarters

MOULD
4 x 150 ml (5 fl oz) moulds and 4 x 100 ml (3½ fl oz) moulds

---

1 To prepare the lemon verbena jelly, combine the sugar syrup, lemon juice and lemon verbena with 150 ml (5 fl oz) water in a small saucepan, and heat gently over low heat for 5 minutes. Remove from the heat and set aside for 10–15 minutes, to infuse and cool.

2 Meanwhile, to prepare the lemon verbena and mint blancmange, combine the milk, sugar syrup, lemon verbena and mint in a small saucepan and heat gently over low heat for 5 minutes. Remove from the heat and set aside for 10–15 minutes, to infuse and cool.

3 Once cool, strain the liquids separately through a muslin-lined sieve into medium-sized heatproof bowls (rinse the cloth between each batch). Add the gelatine to each mixture and set aside for 5–10 minutes, until the gelatine has softened.

4 Set each bowl over a saucepan of simmering water and heat gently, stirring occasionally, until the gelatine dissolves. Remove from the heat and set aside to cool.

5 Strain the liquids separately through a muslin-lined sieve (rinse the cloth between each batch). Cover the lemon verbena and mint mixture and keep at room temperature until required.

6 Place the larger moulds onto a tray and pour 2½ tablespoons (50 ml/1¾ fl oz) of the lemon verbena mixture into each mould. Place the smaller moulds on top of the liquid, and fill with pie weights, dried beans or rice, until the lemon verbena mixture rises up to fill the space between the two moulds. Centre the mould and place two strips of sticky tape over the top to hold in place. Refrigerate for 30–45 minutes, until firm set.

CONTINUED

7   When the outer jelly is set, remove the tape and discard the weights. Half-fill the inner mould with hot water and leave for 10–15 seconds, to soften the surface of the jelly below. Place your fingers inside the inner mould and gently twist and lift, until the mould is released. Refrigerate for 10 minutes, or until the jelly re-sets but is still slightly tacky when touched.

8   Pour in the lemon verbena and mint mixture, filling so it is level with the top of the outside jelly layer. Refrigerate for 2 hours, or until firm set.

9   Unmould to serve.

SERVES 4

Extra lemon verbena jelly mixture has been allocated in this recipe to allow for spills and topping up.

Poached Pear & Moscato

- 1½ cups (330 g/11½ oz) sugar
- 2 small firm pears (such as baby corella), peeled and stems removed
- 2½ cups (625 ml/21 fl oz) moscato
- 4½ leaves titanium-strength gelatine, cut into quarters

MOULD

2 x 1½ cup (375 ml/12½ fl oz) moulds

1   Combine the sugar with 1½ cups (375 ml/12½ fl oz) water in a small saucepan and heat gently over low heat, stirring occasionally, until the sugar dissolves.

2   Meanwhile, using a small teaspoon or melon baller, scoop out the pear cores, leaving the tops intact. Place the pears into the sugar syrup and cover with a round of baking paper. Poach for 15–20 minutes, until just tender. Remove from the heat and set aside, leaving the pears to cool in the poaching liquid.

3   Combine the moscato and ½ cup (125 ml/4 fl oz) of the pear-poaching liquid in a medium-sized bowl.

4   Place the gelatine in a medium-sized heatproof bowl and pour in just enough moscato mixture to cover. Set aside for 5–10 minutes, until the gelatine has softened.

5   Set the bowl over a saucepan of simmering water and heat gently, stirring occasionally, until the gelatine dissolves. Remove from the heat, add the remaining moscato mixture and stir to combine.

6   Strain through a muslin-lined sieve.

7   Divide one quarter of the moscato mixture between the moulds and skim off any bubbles. Refrigerate for 15–20 minutes, until semi set.

CONTINUED

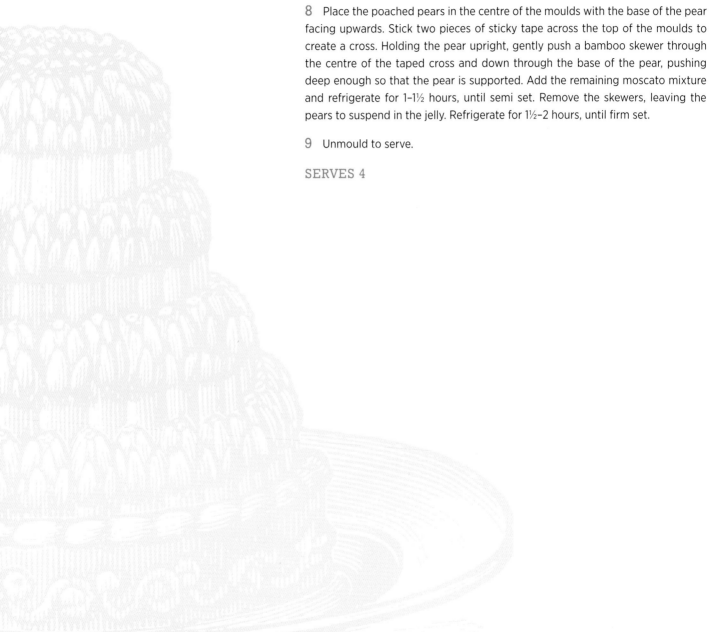

8   Place the poached pears in the centre of the moulds with the base of the pear facing upwards. Stick two pieces of sticky tape across the top of the moulds to create a cross. Holding the pear upright, gently push a bamboo skewer through the centre of the taped cross and down through the base of the pear, pushing deep enough so that the pear is supported. Add the remaining moscato mixture and refrigerate for 1–1½ hours, until semi set. Remove the skewers, leaving the pears to suspend in the jelly. Refrigerate for 1½–2 hours, until firm set.

9   Unmould to serve.

SERVES 4

Prosecco and Violet

- 3 leaves titanium-strength gelatine, cut into quarters
- ⅓ cup (75 g/2½ oz) sugar
- ⅓ cup (80 ml/3 fl oz) violet syrup
- 1½ tablespoons (30 ml/1 fl oz) freshly squeezed lemon juice
- 1 x 750 ml (25 fl oz) bottle prosecco, chilled in the freezer for 30 minutes

---

MOULD
any – total capacity of 3 cups (750 ml/25 fl oz)

This recipe doesn't use the entire bottle of prosecco. Serve the left-over wine with the jelly, or perhaps enjoy a glass or two while you are waiting for it to set.

1 Place the gelatine in a small bowl. Cover with cold water and set aside for 5–10 minutes, until the gelatine has softened.

2 Combine the sugar with ⅓ cup (80 ml/3 fl oz) water in a small saucepan and heat gently over low heat, stirring occasionally, until the sugar dissolves. Remove from the heat.

3 When the gelatine has softened, drain the water and squeeze any excess liquid from the gelatine. Add to the sugar syrup and stir, until the gelatine dissolves. Add the violet syrup and lemon juice, and stir to combine. Transfer to a medium-sized bowl and set aside to cool.

4 Set the bowl of violet mixture into a bowl of iced water and stir continuously, until it thickens.

5 Slowly add 2 cups (500 ml/17 fl oz) of the chilled prosecco, pouring it against the inside of the bowl to prevent excess froth. Stir to combine.

6 Strain the liquid through a muslin-lined sieve and skim off any froth.

7 Pour the prosecco mixture into the mould, pouring the liquid down against the inside of the mould to prevent excess froth. Skim off any bubbles and refrigerate for 4–6 hours, until firm set.

8 Unmould to serve.

SERVES 4

Rosé and Raspberry

- 6 leaves titanium-strength gelatine
  (7 leaves if setting in a single large mould),
  cut into quarters
- 1 cup (250 ml/8½ fl oz) sugar syrup (page 7)
- 1 x 750 ml (25 fl oz) bottle rosé, chilled
- 125 g (4½ oz) raspberries, washed

MOULD
any – total capacity of 4 cups (1 L /34 fl oz)

This jelly also looks lovely served in glasses, as pictured. If you don't want to unmould your jelly, it should be soft set, which requires less gelatine. Refer to the conversion chart on page 5.

1   Place the gelatine in a large heatproof bowl. Add the sugar syrup and set aside for 5–10 minutes, until the gelatine has softened.

2   Set the bowl over a saucepan of simmering water and heat gently, stirring occasionally, until the gelatine dissolves. Remove from the heat and slowly add the rosé, stirring to combine.

3   Strain through a muslin-lined sieve and skim off any bubbles.

4   Scatter the raspberries over the base of the mould and pour in enough rosé mixture to just cover the raspberries. Skim off any bubbles and refrigerate for 5–15 minutes, until semi set.

5   Add the remaining rosé mixture, pouring slowly over the back of a dessert spoon resting against the inside of the mould. Skim off any bubbles and refrigerate for 2–6 hours, until firm set.

6   Unmould to serve.

SERVES 8

Champagne Posy

- 6 leaves titanium-strength gelatine (7 leaves if setting in a single large mould), cut into quarters
- ½ cup (110 g/4 oz) sugar
- 1 x 750 ml (25 fl oz) bottle Champagne or sparkling white wine, chilled in the freezer for 30 minutes
- 1–2 cups organic edible flowers (such as pansies, violets or peonies), pistils and stamens removed

---

MOULD
any – total capacity of 4 cups (1 L/34 fl oz)

1   Place the gelatine in a small bowl and cover with cold water. Set aside for 5–10 minutes, until the gelatine has softened.

2   Combine the sugar with ½ cup (125 ml/4 fl oz) water in a small saucepan and heat gently over low heat, stirring occasionally, until the sugar dissolves. Remove from the heat.

3   When the gelatine has softened, drain the water and squeeze any excess liquid from the gelatine. Add to the sugar syrup and stir until the gelatine has dissolved. Transfer to a large bowl and set aside for 10 minutes, to cool.

4   Set the bowl containing the gelatine mixture over a bowl of iced water and stir continuously, until it thickens. Slowly add the chilled wine, pouring it against the inside of the bowl to prevent excess froth. Stir to combine.

5   Strain the liquid through a muslin-lined sieve and skim off any froth.

6   Scatter some flowers over the base of your mould and pour in enough wine mixture to just cover the flowers. Skim off any bubbles and refrigerate for 5–15 minutes, until semi set.

7   Repeat the process, pouring the mixture slowly over the back of a dessert spoon resting against the inside of the mould, to make four more layers. Refrigerate for 2–6 hours, until firm set.

8   Unmould to serve.

SERVES 8

Peach Melba

RASPBERRY JELLY
- 300 g (10½ oz) raspberries
- ¼ cup (55 g/2 oz) sugar
- 4½ leaves gold-strength gelatine, cut into quarters

PEACH JELLY
- 2 tablespoons (40 ml/1½ fl oz) orange juice
- 1 x 400 g (14 oz) tin peach halves in syrup
- 3 leaves gold-strength gelatine, cut into quarters

MOULD
1 x 2 cup (500 ml/17 fl oz) mould

1 To prepare the raspberry jelly, combine the raspberries and sugar with 1 cup (250 ml/8½ fl oz) water in a small saucepan and heat gently over low heat for 5 minutes, or until the raspberries have softened.

2 Strain the raspberries through a muslin-lined sieve into a measuring jug. If necessary, add enough water to make 1½ cups (375 ml/12½ fl oz) in total. Set aside to cool.

3 Meanwhile, to prepare the peach jelly, combine the orange juice with ⅔ cup (160 ml/5½ fl oz) of the peach syrup and 3 tablespoons (60 ml/2 fl oz) water in a bowl. Cut two of the peach halves into slices and set aside.

4 Place the gelatine for both jellies in separate medium-sized heatproof bowls and pour in just enough of the liquids to cover. Set aside for 5–10 minutes, until the gelatine has softened.

5 Set each bowl over a saucepan of simmering water and heat gently, stirring occasionally, until the gelatine dissolves. Remove from the heat, add the remainder of each liquid and stir to combine.

6 Strain the liquids separately through a muslin-lined sieve (rinse the cloth between each batch). Cover the peach mixture and keep at room temperature until required.

7 Pour half the raspberry mixture into the mould and skim off any bubbles. Refrigerate for 30 minutes, or until semi set.

CONTINUED

8 Add one quarter of the peach mixture, pouring slowly over the back of a dessert spoon resting against the inside of the mould. Refrigerate for 10–15 minutes, or until semi set.

9 Place a peach half in the centre of the mould, with the cut side facing upwards, and arrange the peach slices around. Pour in half of the remaining peach mixture, using the back of a spoon as before, and refrigerate for 10–15 minutes, until semi set.

10 Add the remaining peach mixture and refrigerate for 5–10 minutes, until semi set.

11 Add the remaining raspberry mixture, pouring over the back of a spoon as before, and refrigerate for 2–3 hours, until firm set.

12 Unmould to serve.

SERVES 4

Serve the remaining tinned peaches with the jelly, or save them for dessert or breakfast for another day.

Trifle

- 4 mini jam rolls sliced into 1 cm (⅜ in) rounds
- ¾ cup (180 ml/6 fl oz) thickened cream, lightly whipped
- 2 tablespoons flaked almonds, lightly toasted
- 2–3 strawberries, sliced

STRAWBERRY JELLY

- 450 g (1 lb) strawberries, hulled and coarsely chopped
- ¼ cup (55 g/2 oz) sugar
- juice of ½ lemon
- 1 tablespoon (20 ml/¾ fl oz) brandy (optional)
- 3 leaves gold-strength gelatine, cut into quarters

ADVOCAAT BLANCMANGE

- 1 cup (250 ml/8½ fl oz) full-cream milk
- ½ cup (125 ml/4 fl oz) sugar syrup (page 7)
- ½ cup (125 ml/4 fl oz) advocaat
- 4½ leaves gold-strength gelatine, cut into quarters

MOULD
1 x 3 cup (750 ml/25 fl oz) bowl-shaped mould

1   To prepare the strawberry jelly, place the strawberries, sugar and lemon juice in a medium-sized bowl and mash together using a potato masher. Set aside for 30 minutes.

2   Pour the strawberry mixture into a muslin-lined sieve and set aside to strain for about 30 minutes. Occasionally stir gently, but do not scrape or press the mixture through the cloth as this will make the juice cloudy.

3   Meanwhile, to prepare the advocaat blancmange, combine the milk, sugar syrup and advocaat in a medium-sized bowl.

4   Pour the strained strawberry juice into a measuring jug (there should be around 150 ml/5 fl oz of liquid). Add the brandy (if using) and 100 ml (3½ fl oz) water.

5   Place the gelatine for both jellies in separate medium-sized heatproof bowls and pour in just enough of the liquids to cover. Set aside for 5–10 minutes, until the gelatine has softened.

6   Set each bowl over a saucepan of simmering water and heat gently, stirring occasionally, until the gelatine dissolves. Remove from the heat, add the remainder of each liquid and stir to combine.

7   Strain the liquids separately through a muslin-lined sieve (rinse the cloth between each batch). Cover the advocaat blancmange mixture and keep at room temperature until required.

CONTINUED

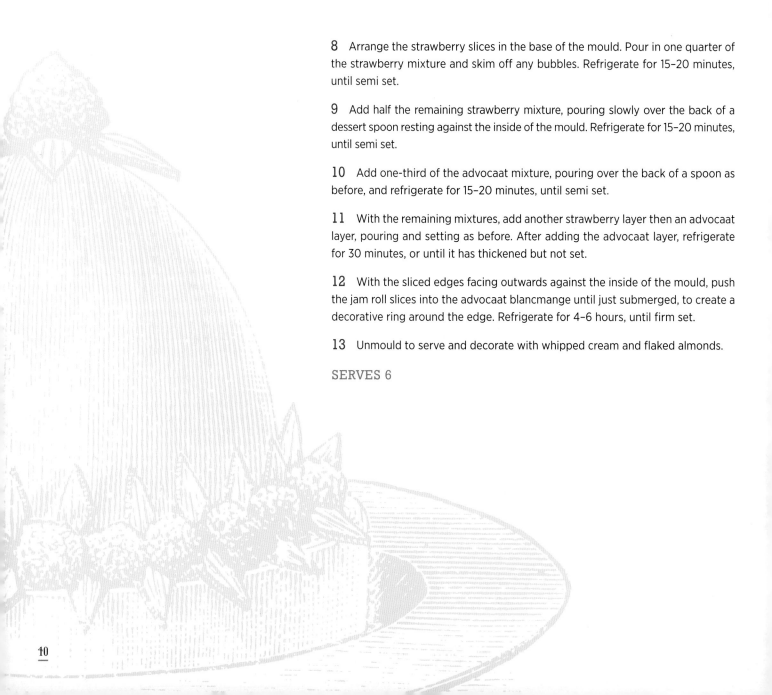

8   Arrange the strawberry slices in the base of the mould. Pour in one quarter of the strawberry mixture and skim off any bubbles. Refrigerate for 15–20 minutes, until semi set.

9   Add half the remaining strawberry mixture, pouring slowly over the back of a dessert spoon resting against the inside of the mould. Refrigerate for 15–20 minutes, until semi set.

10   Add one-third of the advocaat mixture, pouring over the back of a spoon as before, and refrigerate for 15–20 minutes, until semi set.

11   With the remaining mixtures, add another strawberry layer then an advocaat layer, pouring and setting as before. After adding the advocaat layer, refrigerate for 30 minutes, or until it has thickened but not set.

12   With the sliced edges facing outwards against the inside of the mould, push the jam roll slices into the advocaat blancmange until just submerged, to create a decorative ring around the edge. Refrigerate for 4–6 hours, until firm set.

13   Unmould to serve and decorate with whipped cream and flaked almonds.

SERVES 6

Choc Mint Slice

MINT BLANCMANGE

- 1¾ leaves gold-strength gelatine, cut into quarters
- 1 cup (250 ml/8½ fl oz) full-cream milk
- 1 tablespoon (20 ml/¾ fl oz) sugar syrup (page 7)
- 5–10 white mints

CHOCOLATE BLANCMANGE

- 2 leaves gold-strength gelatine, cut into quarters
- 1 cup (250 ml/8½ fl oz) full-cream milk
- 1 tablespoon (20 ml/¾ fl oz) sugar syrup (page 7)
- 50 g (1¾ oz) dark chocolate, coarsely chopped
- 6 plain chocolate biscuits, coarsely crushed

MOULD
4 x ½ cup (125 ml/4 fl oz) moulds

1   Place the gelatine for both jellies into separate bowls. Cover with cold water and set aside for 5–10 minutes, until the gelatine has softened.

2   To prepare the mint blancmange, heat the milk, sugar syrup and mints together in a small saucepan over low heat for 3–5 minutes, until it begins to simmer. Taste, and add a few extra mints if required.

3   To prepare the chocolate blancmange, heat the milk and sugar syrup in a small saucepan over low heat for 3–5 minutes, until it begins to simmer. Remove from the heat, add the chocolate and stir until melted.

4   When the gelatine has softened, drain the water from the bowls and squeeze any excess liquid from the gelatine. Add the gelatine to the blancmange mixtures and stir until the gelatine has dissolved.

5   Strain the liquids separately through a muslin-lined sieve (rinse the cloth between each batch). Cover the mint mixture and keep at room temperature until required.

6   Divide half the chocolate mixture between the moulds and refrigerate for 20–30 minutes, until semi set.

7   Divide the mint mixture between the moulds, pouring over the back of a dessert spoon resting against the inside of the mould. Refrigerate for 30 minutes, until semi set.

8   Stir the crushed biscuits through the remaining chocolate mixture. Divide between the moulds and refrigerate for 1–1½ hours, until firm set.

9   Unmould to serve.

SERVES 4

Tiramisu

- cocoa powder, for dusting

MASCARPONE BLANCMANGE
- ½ cup (125 ml/4 fl oz) sugar syrup (page 7)
- 2½ leaves gold-strength gelatine, cut into quarters
- ¾ cup (180 g/6½ oz) mascarpone cheese

COFFEE JELLY
- ¼ cup (55 g/2 oz) sugar
- 2 shots (60 ml/2 fl oz) espresso coffee
- 3 leaves gold-strength gelatine, cut into quarters

MARSALA BLANCMANGE
- 3 tablespoons (60 ml/2 fl oz) Marsala
- 3 tablespoons (60 ml/2 fl oz) full-cream milk
- 1 leaf gold-strength gelatine, cut into quarters

MOULD
4 x ¾ cup (180 ml/6 fl oz) moulds

1   To prepare the mascarpone blancmange, combine the sugar syrup with ⅓ cup (80 ml/3 fl oz) water in a small heatproof bowl. Add the gelatine and set aside for 5–10 minutes, until the gelatine has softened.

2   Set the bowl over a saucepan of simmering water and heat gently, stirring occasionally, until the gelatine dissolves. Remove from the heat, add the mascarpone and stir to combine. Strain through a fine-mesh sieve into a measuring jug. If necessary, add enough water to make 1½ cups (375 ml/12½ fl oz) in total. Cover and keep at room temperature until required.

3   To prepare the coffee jelly, place the gelatine in a small bowl. Cover with cold water and set aside for 5–10 minutes, until the gelatine has softened. Combine the sugar and coffee with ¾ cup (180 ml/6 fl oz) water in a small saucepan, and heat gently over low heat for 3–5 minutes, stirring occasionally, until the sugar dissolves.

4   When the gelatine has softened, drain the water and squeeze any excess liquid from the gelatine. Add to the coffee mixture and stir until the gelatine has dissolved. Strain the liquid through a muslin-lined sieve into a measuring jug. If necessary, add enough water to make 1 cup (250 ml/8½ fl oz) in total. Cover and keep at room temperature until required.

5   To prepare the Marsala jelly, combine the Marsala and the milk in a small heatproof bowl. Add the gelatine and set aside for 5–10 minutes, until the gelatine has softened.

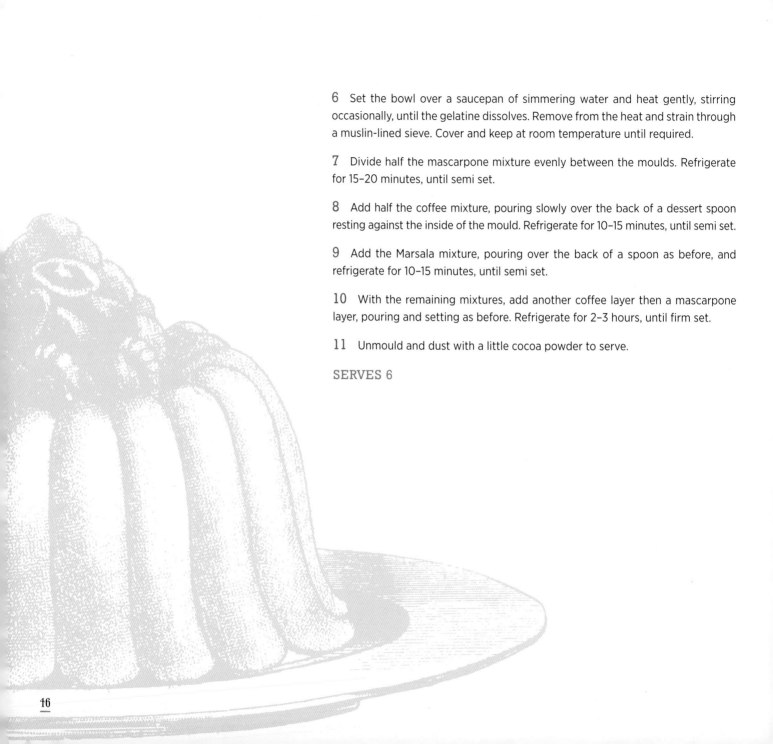

6 Set the bowl over a saucepan of simmering water and heat gently, stirring occasionally, until the gelatine dissolves. Remove from the heat and strain through a muslin-lined sieve. Cover and keep at room temperature until required.

7 Divide half the mascarpone mixture evenly between the moulds. Refrigerate for 15–20 minutes, until semi set.

8 Add half the coffee mixture, pouring slowly over the back of a dessert spoon resting against the inside of the mould. Refrigerate for 10–15 minutes, until semi set.

9 Add the Marsala mixture, pouring over the back of a spoon as before, and refrigerate for 10–15 minutes, until semi set.

10 With the remaining mixtures, add another coffee layer then a mascarpone layer, pouring and setting as before. Refrigerate for 2–3 hours, until firm set.

11 Unmould and dust with a little cocoa powder to serve.

SERVES 6

Cassata

- 2 tablespoons flaked almonds, lightly toasted
- 2 green glacé cherries, sliced
- 2 red glacé cherries, sliced

ALMOND BLANCMANGE

- 2 leaves gold-strength gelatine,
  cut into quarters
- 1 cup (250 ml/8½ fl oz) full-cream milk
- ¾ cup (75 g/2½ oz) almond meal
- 2 tablespoons (40 ml/1½ fl oz) sugar syrup
  (page 7)

RICOTTA & VANILLA BLANCMANGE

- 2 leaves gold-strength gelatine,
  cut into quarters
- ¾ cup (180 ml/6 fl oz) full-cream milk
- ⅓ cup (90 g/3 oz) smooth ricotta
- 2 tablespoons (40 ml/1½ fl oz) sugar syrup
  (page 7)
- ½ vanilla bean, split lengthways

MOULD

1 x 2 cup (500 ml/17 fl oz) mould and
1 x 1 cup (250 ml/8½ fl oz) mould

1 Place the gelatine for both jellies in separate small bowls. Cover with cold water and set aside for 5–10 minutes, until the gelatine has softened.

2 Combine the remaining ingredients in separate small saucepans and heat gently over low heat for 5 minutes. Remove from the heat.

3 When the gelatine has softened, drain the water and squeeze any excess liquid from the gelatine. Add to the mixtures and stir until the gelatine has dissolved. Set aside for 10 minutes, to cool slightly.

4 Strain the ricotta mixture through a fine-mesh sieve placed over a jug. Scrape the mixture through the sieve with a spoon, to remove any lumps. Cover and keep at room temperature until required. (The mixture will thicken to the consistency of thick custard. If it sets too much and becomes lumpy, warm it over a saucepan of simmering water and stir until it becomes smooth again.)

5 Strain the almond mixture through a muslin-lined sieve.

6 Place the larger mould on a tray and pour in the almond mixture. Place the smaller mould on top of the liquid, and fill with pie weights, dried beans or rice, until the almond mixture rises up to fill the space between the two moulds. Centre the mould and place two strips of sticky tape over the top to hold in place. Refrigerate for 1 hour, or until firm set.

7   When the outer jelly is set, remove the tape and discard the weights. Half-fill the inner mould with hot water and leave for 10–15 seconds, to soften the surface of the jelly below. Place your fingers inside the inner mould and gently twist and lift, until the mould is released. Refrigerate for 10 minutes, or until the jelly re-sets, but is still slightly tacky when touched.

8   Add the almonds and cherries to the ricotta mixture and stir until the cherries have turned the blancmange a pale peach colour. Pour into the centre of the mould and refrigerate for 4 hours, or until firm set.

9   Unmould to serve.

SERVES 4

Persian Delight

- Persian fairy floss, to decorate

PISTACHIO BLANCMANGE

- ¾ cup (90g/3oz) unsalted, shelled pistachio nuts
- 1 cup (250ml/8½ fl oz) full-cream milk
- 2½ leaves gold-strength gelatine, cut into quarters
- 3 tablespoons (60ml/2fl oz) sugar syrup (page 7)

ROSEWATER BLANCMANGE

- 1⅓ leaves gold-strength gelatine, cut into quarters
- ⅓ cup (80ml/3fl oz) sugar syrup (page 7)
- 100ml (3½ fl oz) full-cream milk
- 1 teaspoon rosewater
- 1–3 drops pink food colouring

MOULD
any – total capacity of 2 cups (500ml/17fl oz)

1　To prepare the pistachio blancmange, blanch the pistachios for 10 seconds in boiling water, then plunge into iced water to cool. Drain, and rub the pistachios in your hands to remove the skins. Place the pistachios in a small food-processor and blend, until finely ground. Combine with ¾ cup (180ml/6fl oz) of the milk in a small saucepan and heat over low for 10 minutes. Remove from the heat and set aside for 10 minutes.

2　Place the gelatine for both jellies in separate heatproof bowls. For the pistachio, add the remaining milk and the sugar syrup. For the rosewater, add the sugar syrup and milk. Set aside for 5–10 minutes, until the gelatine has softened.

3　Set each bowl over a saucepan of simmering water and heat gently, stirring occasionally, until the gelatine dissolves. Remove from the heat. To the rosewater jelly bowl, add the rosewater and enough food colouring to dye the mixture a soft pink. Add the pistachio-infused milk to the pistachio blancmange bowl and stir to combine.

4　Strain the liquids separately through a muslin-lined sieve (rinse the cloth between each batch). Cover the pistachio mixture and keep at room temperature until required.

5　Pour two-thirds of the rosewater mixture into the mould and skim off any bubbles. Refrigerate for 15–20 minutes, until semi set.

6　Add the pistachio mixture, pouring slowly over the back of a dessert spoon resting against the inside of the mould. Refrigerate for 15–20 minutes, until semi set.

7　Add the remaining rosewater mixture, pouring over the back of a spoon as before, and refrigerate for 2–4 hours, until firm set.

8　Unmould and decorate with Persian fairy floss to serve.

SERVES 4

Pomegranate, Orange and Cardamom Bombe

POMEGRANATE JELLY
- 1 cup pomegranate seeds
- ⅓ cup (80 ml/3 fl oz) sugar syrup (page 7)
- 3½ leaves gold-strength gelatine, cut into quarters

ORANGE & CARDAMOM JELLY
- 1¼ cup (310 ml/10½ fl oz) orange juice
- ½ cup (125 ml/4 fl oz) sugar syrup (page 7)
- 1 teaspoon cardamom pods
- 4½ leaves gold-strength gelatine, cut into quarters

MOULD
4 x 150 ml (5 fl oz) moulds and
4 x 100 ml (3½ fl oz) moulds

1   To prepare the pomegranate jelly, place the pomegranate seeds in a small saucepan and mash gently using a potato masher, to release the juice (be careful, as the juice tends to squirt and will stain your clothes – it helps to cover the saucepan with a dark-coloured tea towel as you mash). Heat gently over low heat for 3–5 minutes, until the juice begins to simmer.

2   Strain through a muslin-lined sieve set over a measuring jug (there should be approximately 150 ml/5 fl oz of juice). Squeeze the muslin to extract all of the juice. Add the sugar syrup then top up with water to make 300 ml (10 fl oz) in total.

3   Place the gelatine in a medium-sized heatproof bowl and pour in just enough pomegranate mixture to cover. Set aside for 5–10 minutes, until the gelatine has softened.

4   Set the bowl over a saucepan of simmering water and heat gently, stirring occasionally, until the gelatine dissolves. Add the remaining pomegranate mixture and stir to combine. Strain through a muslin-lined sieve.

5   To prepare the orange and cardamom jelly, place the gelatine in a small bowl and pour in just enough water to cover. Set aside for 5–10 minutes, until the gelatine has softened. Combine the orange juice, sugar syrup and cardamom seeds in a small saucepan over low heat and simmer gently for 5 minutes. Remove from the heat.

CONTINUED

6   Drain the water from the gelatine bowl and squeeze any excess liquid from the gelatine. Add to the orange and cardamom liquid and stir until the gelatine has dissolved. Strain through a muslin-lined sieve. Cover and keep at room temperature until required.

7   Place the larger moulds on a tray and pour about 3 tablespoons (60 ml/2 fl oz) of the pomegranate mixture into each mould. Place the smaller moulds on top of the liquid, and fill with pie weights, dried beans or rice, until the pomegranate mixture rises up to fill the space between the two moulds. Centre the mould and place two strips of sticky tape over the top to hold in place. Top up the outer mould with additional mixture if required. Refrigerate for 30–45 minutes, until firm set.

8   When the outer jelly is set, remove the tape and discard the weights. Half-fill the inner mould with hot water and leave for 10–15 seconds, to soften the surface of the jelly below. Place your fingers inside the inner mould and gently twist and lift, until the mould is released. Refrigerate for 10 minutes, or until the jelly re-sets, but is still slightly tacky when touched.

9   Pour the orange and cardamom mixture into the centre of the moulds, filling so it is level with the outside jelly layer. Skim off any bubbles. Refrigerate for 2 hours, or until firm set.

10   Unmould to serve.

SERVES 4

The recipe makes a little more pomegranate jelly than is required, to allow for spills and topping up. If you have leftover pomegranate mixture and there is space in the moulds, pour a final layer of pomegranate over the top of the bombe, so that it completely encases the orange jelly on the inside.

Spiced Plum and Cinnamon

SPICED PLUM JELLY
- 500 g (1 lb 2 oz) dark plums (such as Doris or blood), pitted and coarsely chopped
- ¼ cup (55 g/2 oz) sugar
- 3 star anise
- 3¾ leaves gold-strength gelatine, cut into quarters

CINNAMON BLANCMANGE
- 150 ml (5 fl oz) full-cream milk
- 1½ tablespoons (30 ml/1 fl oz) sugar syrup (page 7)
- ½ cinnamon stick
- 1¼ leaves gold-strength gelatine, cut into quarters

MOULD
any – total capacity of 2 cups (500 ml/17 fl oz)

1   To prepare the spiced plum jelly, combine the plums, sugar and star anise with ½ cup (125 ml/4 fl oz) water in a medium saucepan. Simmer over low heat for 10–15 minutes, until plums soften and lose their shape.

2   Spoon the stewed plums into a muslin-lined sieve and set aside to strain for about 15 minutes. Occasionally stir gently, but do not scrape or press the mixture through the cloth as this will make the juice cloudy.

3   Pour the strained plum juice into a measuring jug (there should be approximately 1 cup/250 ml/8½ fl oz of liquid). Add enough water to make 1¼ cups (310 ml/10½ fl oz) in total. Set aside to cool.

4   To prepare the cinnamon blancmange, combine the milk, sugar syrup and cinnamon in a small saucepan and heat gently over low heat for 3–5 minutes, until it begins to simmer. Remove from the heat and set aside for 10 minutes, to infuse and cool.

5   Place the gelatine for both jellies in separate medium-sized heatproof bowls and pour in just enough of the cooled liquids to cover. Set aside for 5–10 minutes, until the gelatine has softened.

6   Set each bowl over a saucepan of simmering water and heat gently, stirring occasionally, until the gelatine dissolves. Remove from the heat, add the remainder of each liquid and stir to combine.

CONTINUED

7 Strain the liquids separately through a muslin-lined sieve (rinse the cloth between each batch). Cover the cinnamon mixture and keep at room temperature until required.

8 Pour the spiced plum mixture into the mould and skim off any bubbles. Refrigerate for 1 hour, until semi set.

9 Add the cinnamon mixture, pouring slowly over the back of a dessert spoon resting against the inside of the mould. Skim off any bubbles. Refrigerate for 2–3 hours, until firm set.

10 Unmould to serve.

SERVES 4

Mulled Wine

MULLED WINE JELLY

- 9 leaves gold-strength gelatine
  (10 leaves if setting in a single large mould),
  cut into quarters
- 1 x 750 ml (25 fl oz) bottle medium–full-bodied
  red wine, such as cabernet sauvignon, shiraz
  or merlot
- ¾ cup (170 g/6 oz) sugar
- juice of ½ an orange
- 1 cinnamon stick
- 2 strips orange zest
- 5 cloves
- 3 black peppercorns
- ⅛ teaspoon finely grated fresh nutmeg or
  ground nutmeg

CINNAMON CREAM

- 1½ cups (375 ml/12½ fl oz) pouring cream
- 1 tablespoon (10 g/⅜ oz) icing sugar
- ½ teaspoon ground cinnamon

MOULD

any – total capacity of 3 cups (750 ml/25 fl oz)

1   To make the mulled wine jelly, place the gelatine in a small bowl and pour in just enough wine to cover. Set aside for 5–10 minutes, until the gelatine has softened.

2   Meanwhile, combine the remaining ingredients in a medium-sized saucepan and heat gently over low heat, stirring occasionally, for 10 minutes, or until the flavours have infused. Remove from the heat, add the softened gelatine mixture and stir occasionally until the gelatine dissolves.

3   Strain through a muslin-lined sieve and set aside to cool.

4   Pour the wine mixture into the mould and skim off any bubbles. Refrigerate for 4 hours, or until firm set.

5   Meanwhile, to make the cinnamon cream, whip the cream, icing sugar and cinnamon together in a medium-sized bowl, until soft peaks form. Cover and refrigerate until required.

6   Unmould and serve with the cinnamon cream.

SERVES 6

Soy Chai Latte

- ground nutmeg, to garnish

CHAI JELLY

- 2 cups (500 ml/17 fl oz) soy milk
- 2½ tablespoons honey
- ½ tablespoon loose black tea
  or 1 tea bag
- 1 cinnamon stick, broken
- 6 cardamom pods, bruised
- 5 whole black peppercorns, crushed
- 4 whole cloves
- ½ teaspoon ground ginger
- ¼ teaspoon finely grated fresh nutmeg
  or ground nutmeg
- ½ teaspoon agar agar powder

SOY MILK JELLY

- 1 cup (250 ml/8½ fl oz) soy milk
- 3 tablespoons (60 ml/2 fl oz) sugar syrup
  (page 7)
- ¼ teaspoon agar agar powder

MOULD
any – total capacity of 3 cups (750 ml/25 fl oz)

1   To prepare the chai jelly, combine all the ingredients except the agar agar in a small saucepan and heat gently over low heat for 10 minutes. Remove from the heat and set aside for 10 minutes to infuse.

2   To prepare the soy milk jelly, combine the soy milk and sugar syrup in a small saucepan, sprinkle with agar agar powder and set aside for 5 minutes, to soften.

3   Strain the chai mixture through a muslin-lined sieve. Rinse the saucepan and return the mixture to the pan. Sprinkle with the agar agar and set aside for 5 minutes, to soften.

4   Place the soy mixture over medium heat and bring to the boil. Stir constantly for 3–5 minutes, to dissolve the agar agar. Pour into the mould and set aside. The jelly will begin to set straight away, but won't set too quickly if kept at room temperature.

5   Place the chai mixture over medium heat and bring to the boil. Stir constantly for 3–5 minutes, to dissolve the agar agar. Set aside to cool slightly.

6   Lightly scrape the surface of the soy jelly with the tines of a fork then pour the chai mixture on top. Refrigerate for 2 hours, or until firm set.

7   Unmould and sprinkle with a little ground nutmeg to serve.

SERVES 4

For extra fun, reverse the order of the layers and serve the jelly in latte glasses instead of unmoulded.

Green Tea and Black Sesame

BLACK SESAME JELLY

- 1½ leaves gold-strength gelatine,
  cut into quarters
- 3 tablespoons black sesame seeds
- 3 tablespoons (60 ml/2 fl oz) sugar syrup
  (page 7)

GREEN TEA BLANCMANGE

- 3 leaves gold-strength gelatine,
  cut into quarters
- ⅓ cup (80 ml/3 fl oz) sugar syrup (page 7)
- 1½ cups (375 ml/12½ fl oz) full-cream milk
- 2 teaspoons green tea powder (matcha)

MOULD
any – total capacity of 600 ml (20 fl oz)

Green tea powder, also known as matcha, is available from Japanese grocers.

1   Place the gelatine for both jellies in separate medium-sized heatproof bowls. For the black sesame jelly, add ½ cup (125 ml/4 fl oz) water. For the green tea blancmange, add the sugar syrup and 3 tablespoons (60 ml/2 fl oz) of the milk. Set aside for 5–10 minutes, until the gelatine has softened.

2   Meanwhile, place the sesame seeds in a small frying pan and cook over low heat for 3–4 minutes, until lightly toasted. Transfer to a mortar and pestle or spice grinder, and grind to a fine powder. Return the sesame seeds to the pan, add the sugar syrup and heat gently over low heat for 3–5 minutes, until the sugar syrup starts to take on colour from the sesame. Remove from the heat and set aside to cool.

3   When the gelatine has softened, set each bowl over a saucepan of simmering water and heat gently, stirring occasionally, until the gelatine dissolves. Remove from the heat, add the remaining ingredients to each bowl and stir to combine.

4   Strain the liquids separately through a muslin-lined sieve (rinse the cloth between each batch). Cover the green tea mixture and keep at room temperature until required.

5   Pour the black sesame mixture into the mould and refrigerate for 10–15 minutes, until semi set.

6   Add the green tea mixture, pouring slowly over the back of a dessert spoon resting against the inside of the mould. Refrigerate for 2–3 hours, until firm set.

7   Unmould to serve.

SERVES 6

Lychee

- 1 x 565 g (1 lb 4 oz) tin lychees in syrup
- 3 tablespoons (60 ml/2 fl oz) sugar syrup (page 7)
- 1½ tablespoons (30 ml/1 fl oz) freshly squeezed lime juice
- 3 leaves titanium-strength gelatine, cut into quarters

MOULD
8 x ½ cup (125 ml/4 fl oz) moulds

1   Strain the lychee syrup into a large measuring jug. Set the lychees aside. Add the sugar syrup and lime juice to the jug and top up with water to make 2 cups (500 ml/17 fl oz) in total.

2   Place the gelatine into a medium-sized heatproof bowl and pour in just enough lychee mixture to cover. Set aside for 5–10 minutes, until the gelatine has softened.

3   Set the bowl over a saucepan of simmering water and heat gently, stirring occasionally, until the gelatine dissolves. Add the remaining lychee mixture and stir to combine.

4   Strain the liquid through a muslin-lined sieve.

5   Pour a little of the lychee liquid into each mould, just enough to cover the bottom. Refrigerate for 10–15 minutes, until semi set.

6   Place a lychee in each mould, then fill with the remaining lychee liquid. Refrigerate for 2–2½ hours, until firm set.

7   Unmould to serve.

MAKES 8

Mandarin and Vanilla

- 3 leaves titanium-strength gelatine, cut into quarters
- ¼ cup (55 g/1¾ fl oz) sugar
- ½ vanilla bean, halved lengthways
- 1 cup (250 ml/8½ fl oz) mandarin juice
- 1–2 mandarins, broken into segments and membrane removed

MOULD
1 x 2 cup (500 ml/17 fl oz) mould

Tinned mandarin segments can be substituted if mandarins are out of season.

1   Place the gelatine into a medium-sized heatproof bowl with ½ cup (125 ml/4 fl oz) water. Set aside for 5–10 minutes, until the gelatine has softened.

2   Combine the sugar and vanilla bean with ½ cup (125 ml/4 fl oz) water in a small saucepan and heat gently over low heat, stirring occasionally, for 3–5 minutes, until the sugar has dissolved. Remove from the heat and set aside for 10 minutes, to infuse.

3   When the gelatine has softened, set the bowl over a saucepan of simmering water and heat gently, stirring occasionally, until the gelatine dissolves. Remove from the heat, pour in the vanilla sugar syrup and the mandarin juice, and stir to combine.

4   Strain through a muslin-lined sieve.

5   Place the bowl containing the mandarin mixture into a large bowl of iced water. Stir continuously until the mixture cools and begins to thicken. Add the mandarin segments and stir to disperse; they should suspend in the jelly mixture rather than sink to the bottom.

6   Pour into the mould and refrigerate for 4 hours, or until firm set.

7   Unmould to serve.

SERVES 4

Blueberry & Elderflower

- 3 leaves titanium-strength gelatine, cut into quarters
- 100 ml (3½ fl oz) sugar syrup (page 7)
- ⅓ cup (80 ml/3 fl oz) dry white wine, such as sauvignon blanc
- ⅓ cup (80 ml/3 fl oz) elderflower cordial
- 2 tablespoons (40 ml/1½ fl oz) freshly squeezed lemon juice
- 125 g (4½ oz) fresh blueberries, washed

MOULD
any – total capacity of 3 cups (750 ml/25 fl oz)

If you're looking for a little extra kick, substitute St Germaine elderflower liqueur for the cordial.

1 Place the gelatine into a medium-sized heatproof bowl with 200 ml (7 fl oz) water. Set aside for 5–10 minutes, until the gelatine has softened.

2 Meanwhile, combine the sugar syrup, wine, elderflower cordial and lemon juice in a small bowl.

3 When the gelatine has softened, set the bowl over a saucepan of simmering water and heat gently, stirring occasionally, until the gelatine dissolves. Add the elderflower mixture and stir to combine.

4 Strain through a muslin-lined sieve.

5 Place the bowl containing the elderflower mixture into a large bowl of iced water. Stir continuously until the mixture cools and begins to thicken. Add the blueberries and stir to disperse; they should suspend in the jelly mixture rather than sink to the bottom.

6 Pour the mixture into the mould and skim off any bubbles. Refrigerate for 3–4 hours, until firm set.

7 Unmould to serve.

SERVES 4–6

Coconut & Mango

- 250 g (9 oz) mango flesh
- 1 x 400 ml (13½ fl oz) tin coconut milk
- ½ cup (125 ml/4 fl oz) sugar syrup (page 7)
- 2 tablespoons (40 ml/1½ fl oz) freshly squeezed lime juice
- 1¾ teaspoon agar agar powder

MOULD
any – total capacity of 3 cups (750 ml/25 fl oz)

1   Place the mango flesh in a food processor or blender and blend to a smooth pulp.

2   Combine the coconut milk, sugar syrup and lime juice with ¾ cup (180 ml/6 fl oz) water in a medium-sized bowl.

3   Pour 1½ cups (375 ml/12½ fl oz) of the coconut mixture into a separate medium-sized bowl. Add the mango pulp and stir to combine. Strain through a fine-mesh sieve into a small saucepan, scraping the mixture through the sieve with the back of a spoon, to break up the fibres. Sprinkle ¾ teaspoon of the agar agar powder over the top and set aside for 5 minutes to soften.

4   Strain the remaining coconut milk mixture through a fine-mesh sieve into a separate small saucepan. Sprinkle with the remaining agar agar powder and set aside for 5 minutes to soften.

5   Place the coconut mixture over medium heat and bring to the boil. Stir constantly for 3–5 minutes, to dissolve the agar agar. Pour into the mould and set aside. The jelly will begin to set straight away, but won't set too quickly if kept at room temperature.

CONTINUED

6   Place the mango mixture over medium heat and bring to the boil. Stir constantly for 3–5 minutes, to dissolve the agar agar. Set aside to cool slightly.

7   Lightly scrape the surface of the coconut jelly with the tines of a fork and pour the warm mango mixture on top. Refrigerate for 2 hours, or until set firmly.

8   Unmould to serve.

SERVES 4–6

Stained Glass

BLUEBERRY JELLY

- 200 g (7 oz) blueberries
- 2 tablespoons (30 g/1 oz) sugar
- 3 leaves gold-strength gelatine, cut into quarters

RASPBERRY JELLY

- 200 g (7 oz) raspberries
- 2 tablespoons (30 g/1 oz) sugar
- 3 leaves gold-strength gelatine, cut into quarters

LEMON JELLY

- ½ cup (125 ml/4 fl oz) freshly squeezed lemon juice
- ½ cup (125 ml/4 fl oz) sugar syrup (page 7)
- 2 tablespoons (40 ml/1½ fl oz) orange juice
- 3 leaves gold-strength gelatine, cut into quarters

BUTTERMILK BLANCMANGE

- 2½ cups (625 ml/21 fl oz) buttermilk
- ½ cup (125 ml/4 fl oz) sugar syrup (page 7)
- 3 leaves gold-strength gelatine, cut into quarters

MOULD
1 x 5 cup (1.25 L/2 pt 10 fl oz) terrine tin

1   To prepare the blueberry and raspberry jellies, combine the berries and sugar in separate saucepans, add ¾ cup (180 ml/6 fl oz) water to each and heat gently over low heat for 5 minutes, or until the berries have softened.

2   Strain the berries separately through a muslin-lined sieve into a measuring jug. Add enough water to make 1 cup (250 ml/8½ fl oz) of each liquid. Set aside to cool.

3   Meanwhile, to prepare the lemon jelly, combine the lemon juice, sugar syrup and orange juice in a bowl.

4   Place the gelatine for the blueberry, raspberry and lemon jellies in separate medium-sized heatproof bowls and pour in just enough of the liquids to cover. Set aside for 5-10 minutes, until the gelatine has softened.

5   Set each bowl over a saucepan of simmering water and heat gently, stirring occasionally, until the gelatine dissolves. Remove from the heat, add the remainder of each liquid and stir to combine.

6   Strain the liquids separately through a muslin-lined sieve (rinse the cloth between each batch).

7   Pour the mixtures into separate 2 cup (500 ml/17 fl oz) capacity square plastic containers and refrigerate for 1½-2 hours, until firm set.

CONTINUED

8 Meanwhile, to prepare the buttermilk blancmange, combine the buttermilk and sugar syrup in a medium-sized bowl. Place the gelatine in a small heatproof bowl, pour in just enough of the buttermilk mixture to cover and set aside for 5–10 minutes, until the gelatine has softened.

9 Set the bowl over a saucepan of simmering water and heat gently, stirring occasionally, until the gelatine dissolves. Remove from the heat, add the remaining buttermilk mixture and stir to combine.

10 Strain through a muslin-lined sieve.

11 Unmould the blueberry, raspberry and lemon jellies and cut into even-sized cubes using a hot thin-bladed knife.

12 Set the bowl containing the buttermilk mixture into a large bowl of iced water. Stir continuously until the mixture cools and begins to thicken. Add the jelly cubes and stir to disperse; they should suspend in the jelly mixture rather than sink to the bottom.

13 Pour the mixture into the terrine mould and refrigerate for 4–6 hours, until firm set.

14 Unmould and serve sliced to reveal the stained glass effect.

SERVES 8–10

Substitute full-cream milk combined with 2 teaspoons freshly squeezed lemon juice for the buttermilk, if unavailable.

Saffron Gold

- 4⅓ leaves titanium-strength gelatine, cut into quarters
- pinch of saffron threads
- 3 tablespoons (60 ml/2 fl oz) honey
- 3 tablespoons (60 ml/2 fl oz) sugar syrup (page 7)
- 4–8 sheets edible gold leaf (optional)

MOULD

any – total capacity of 3 cups (750 ml/25 fl oz)

Edible gold leaf is available from specialty food and cake decorating supply stores.

1   Place the gelatine into a medium-sized heatproof bowl with the saffron and 1 cup (250 ml/8½ fl oz) water. Set aside for 5–10 minutes, until the gelatine has softened.

2   Set the bowl over a saucepan of simmering water and heat gently, stirring occasionally, until the gelatine dissolves. Add the honey and stir until melted and combined. Pour in the sugar syrup and 1½ cups (375 ml/12½ fl oz) water, and stir to combine.

3   Strain through a muslin-lined sieve.

4   If using gold leaf, use tweezers to drop the leaves into the saffron and honey mixture. Whisk lightly, to break the leaves into fragments. Set over a bowl of iced water and stir continuously until the mixture cools and begins to thicken; the gold leaf should suspend in the jelly mixture rather than sink to the bottom.

5   Pour the mixture into the mould and skim off any bubbles. Refrigerate for 4 hours, until firm set.

6   Unmould to serve.

SERVES 4–6

Raspberry, Goat's Cheese & Basil

BASIL JELLY

- 2 cups firmly packed fresh basil leaves,
  plus extra to decorate
- 1 tablespoon (15 g/½ oz) sugar
- 1¼ leaves gold-strength gelatine,
  cut into quarters

RASPBERRY JELLY

- 150 g (5 oz) raspberries
- 2 teaspoons sugar
- 2 leaves gold-strength gelatine,
  cut into quarters

GOAT'S CHEESE BLANCMANGE

- ¾ leaf gold-strength gelatine,
  cut into quarters
- 100 ml (3½ fl oz) goat's milk
  (or full-cream cow's milk)
- 150 g (5 oz) soft goat's cheese

MOULD
4 x ½ cup (125 ml/4 fl oz) moulds

1   To prepare the basil jelly, combine the basil leaves and sugar with 100 ml (3½ fl oz) water in a small saucepan, and heat gently over low heat, for 2–4 minutes, until the leaves begin to turn brown. Remove from the heat and set aside for 10 minutes, to infuse and cool.

2   Meanwhile, to prepare the raspberry jelly, combine the raspberries and sugar with ⅓ cup (80 ml/3 fl oz) water in a small saucepan and heat gently over low heat for 5 minutes, or until the raspberries have softened.

3   Strain the raspberries through a muslin-lined sieve into a measuring jug. If necessary, add enough water to make ⅔ cup (160 ml/5½ fl oz) in total. Set aside to cool.

4   To prepare the goat's cheese blancmange, place the gelatine in a small bowl. Cover with cold water and set aside for 5–10 minutes, until the gelatine has softened. Combine the milk and the goat's cheese and in a small heatproof bowl and set aside.

5   Place the gelatine for the basil and raspberry jellies in separate medium-sized heatproof bowls and pour in just enough of the liquids to cover. Set aside for 5–10 minutes, until the gelatine has softened. When the gelatine for the goat's cheese blancmange has softened, drain the water, squeeze any excess liquid from the gelatine and add to the goat's cheese mixture.

CONTINUED

6   Set each bowl over a saucepan of simmering water and heat gently, stirring occasionally, until the gelatine dissolves. Remove from the heat and set aside to cool.

7   Strain the basil and raspberry liquids separately through a muslin-lined sieve (rinse the cloth between each batch). Strain the goat's cheese mixture through a fine-mesh sieve, scraping the mixture through with the back of a spoon, to remove any lumps. Cover the raspberry and goat's cheese mixtures and keep at room temperature until required.

8   Place two small basil leaves in the base of each mould. Gently pour in enough basil liquid to just cover and refrigerate for 5 minutes, or until semi set.

9   Divide the remaining basil liquid between the moulds, pouring slowly over the back of a dessert spoon resting against the inside of the mould. Refrigerate for 10–15 minutes, until semi set.

10   Add the goat's cheese mixture, pouring over the back of a spoon as before, and refrigerate for 30 minutes, or until semi set.

11   Add the raspberry mixture, pouring over the back of a spoon as before, and refrigerate for 1–2 hours, until firm set.

SERVES 4–8

Serve as a starter with some delicate salad leaves, such as baby endive, or with crackers as part of a cheese board.

Bloody Mary Shots

CLEAR TOMATO JELLY
- 1 kg (2 lb 3 oz) ripe tomatoes
- 1 teaspoon ground sea salt
- 1 egg white, lightly beaten
- 2 tablespoons (40 ml/1½ fl oz) vodka
- 1½ tablespoons (30 ml/1 fl oz) freshly squeezed lemon juice
- 3 leaves gold-strength gelatine, cut into quarters

RED TOMATO JELLY
- ¾ cup (180 ml/6 fl oz) tomato juice
- 1 tablespoon (20 ml/¾ fl oz) vodka
- 1 teaspoon freshly squeezed lemon juice
- 1–1½ teaspoons Worcestershire sauce
- 2–3 dashes Tabasco sauce
- ¼ teaspoon celery salt
- 1 leaf gold-strength gelatine, cut into quarters

MOULD
6 x 50 ml (1¾ fl oz) shot glasses

1   To prepare the clear tomato jelly, coarsely chop the tomatoes and place in a medium-sized bowl. Sprinkle with the salt and toss to combine. Set aside for about 30 minutes.

2   Transfer the tomato and any liquid to a large muslin-lined sieve and set aside to strain for about 2 hours. Occasionally stir gently, but do not scrape or press the mixture through the cloth as this will make the juice cloudy.

3   Meanwhile, to prepare the red tomato jelly, strain the tomato juice through a muslin-lined sieve into a measuring jug. Add the vodka, and the lemon juice, Worcestershire and Tabasco sauces and celery salt, adjusting quantities to taste. If necessary, top up with water to make ½ cup (125 ml/4 fl oz) in total.

4   Place the gelatine for both jellies in separate small heatproof bowls. For the red tomato jelly, add just enough of the mixture to cover. For the clear tomato jelly, add just enough cold water to cover. Set aside for 5–10 minutes, until the gelatine has softened.

5   Transfer the clear tomato liquid to a small saucepan, add the egg white and whisk to combine. Heat gently over low heat for 3–5 minutes, until the impurities in the juice connect with the egg white and float to the surface (this is called a 'raft'), leaving the remaining liquid a clear, light-golden colour. Skim the raft off the surface and discard. Strain the juice through a muslin-lined sieve into a measuring jug. Add the vodka and lemon juice and stir to combine. If necessary, top up with water to make ¾ cup (180 ml/6 fl oz) in total.

CONTINUED

6   When the gelatine for the clear tomato jelly has softened, drain the water, squeeze any excess liquid from the gelatine, return to the bowl and add the clear tomato mixture.

7   Set each gelatine bowl over a saucepan of simmering water and heat gently, stirring occasionally, until the gelatine dissolves. Remove from the heat and set aside to cool.

8   Strain the liquids separately through a muslin-lined sieve (rinse the cloth between each batch). Cover the red tomato mixture and keep at room temperature until required.

9   Divide the clear tomato liquid evenly between the shot glasses. Refrigerate for 20–25 minutes, until semi set.

10   Add the red tomato mixture, pouring slowly over the back of a teaspoon resting against the inside of the glass. Refrigerate for 1 hour, or until soft set.

SERVES 6

To make a Virgin Mary, omit the vodka and substitute more tomato juice in the red layer and water in the clear layer. For extra extravagance, garnish shots with a little horseradish cream, small cooked prawns, celery and cracked pepper.

Flaming B-52 Shots

• Grand Marnier, to serve

KAHLUA JELLY
• 3 tablespoons (60 ml/2 fl oz) Kahlua
  or other coffee liqueur
• 1 tablespoon (20 ml/¾ fl oz) sugar syrup
  (page 7)
• 1½ leaves gold-strength gelatine,
  cut into quarters

BAILEYS JELLY
• 3 tablespoons (60 ml/2 fl oz) Baileys,
  or other Irish cream liqueur
• 1 tablespoon (20 ml/¾ fl oz) sugar syrup
  (page 7)
• 1½ leaves gold-strength gelatine,
  cut into quarters

GRAND MARNIER JELLY
• 3 tablespoons (60 ml/2 fl oz) Grand Marnier
• 1 tablespoon (20 ml/¾ fl oz) sugar syrup
  (page 7)
• 1½ leaves gold-strength gelatine,
  cut into quarters

MOULD
8 x 50 ml (1¾ fl oz) shot glasses

1   Combine the liquid ingredients for each of the jellies in separate medium-sized heatproof bowls. Add the gelatine and 2 tablespoons (40 ml/1½ fl oz) water to each of the bowls and set aside for 5–10 minutes, until the gelatine has softened.

2   Set each bowl over a saucepan of simmering water and heat gently, stirring occasionally, until the gelatine dissolves.

3   Strain the liquids separately through a muslin-lined sieve (rinse the cloth between each batch). Cover the Baileys and Grand Marnier mixtures and keep at room temperature until required.

4   Divide the Kahlua mixture evenly between the shot glasses. Refrigerate for 10–15 minutes, until semi set.

5   Add the Baileys mixture, pouring slowly over the back of a teaspoon resting against the inside of the glass. Refrigerate for 10–15 minutes, until semi set.

6   Add the Grand Marnier mixture, using the back of a spoon as before, and refrigerate for 1 hour, or until firm set.

7   To serve, add 2 teaspoons of room-temperature Grand Mariner to the top of each shot glass and ignite using a lighter.

SERVES 8

Liquorice Allsort

SAMBUCA JELLY
- 2¼ leaves titanium-strength gelatine, cut into quarters
- ¾ cup (180 ml/6 fl oz) black sambuca (or other aniseed liqueur)
- ¾ cup (180 ml/6 fl oz) sugar syrup (page 7)

YELLOW JELLY
- 3 tablespoons (60 ml/2 fl oz) sugar syrup (page 7)
- 3–4 drops yellow food dye
- ¾ leaf titanium-strength gelatine, cut into quarters

GREEN JELLY
- 3 tablespoons (60 ml/2 fl oz) sugar syrup (page 7)
- 3–4 drops green food dye
- ¾ leaf titanium-strength gelatine, cut into quarters

MOULD
any – total capacity of 3 cups (750 ml/25 fl oz)

Alternatively, set the jelly in a 10 cm x 15 cm (4 in x 6 in) tray. Unmould onto a flat surface lined with a sheet of baking paper and cut into cubes using a heated thin-bladed knife.

1   To prepare the sambuca jelly, place the gelatine in a small bowl. Cover with cold water and set aside for 5–10 minutes, until the gelatine has softened.

2   Combine the liquid ingredients for all the jellies in separate medium-sized heat-proof bowls. Add the gelatine, along with 3 tablespoons (60 ml/2 fl oz) water each, to the yellow and green mixtures and set aside for 5–10 minutes, until the gelatine has softened. When the gelatine for the sambuca jelly has softened, drain the water, squeeze any excess liquid from the gelatine and add to the sambuca mixture.

3   Set each bowl over a saucepan of simmering water and heat gently, stirring occasionally, until the gelatine dissolves.

4   Strain the liquids separately through a muslin-lined sieve (rinse the cloth between each batch). Cover the yellow and green mixtures and keep at room temperature until required.

5   Pour one third of the sambuca mixture into the mould and refrigerate for 30 minutes, or until semi set.

6   Add the yellow mixture, pouring slowly over the back of a dessert spoon resting against the inside of the mould. Refrigerate for 30 minutes, or until semi set.

7   Repeat to create a second sambuca layer, a yellow layer and third sambuca layer. Refrigerate for 2–3 hours, until firm set.

8   Unmould to serve.

SERVES 8

Frangelico and Lime

LIME JELLY
- 3 tablespoons (60 ml/2 fl oz) freshly squeezed lime juice
- 2 tablespoons (40 ml/1½ fl oz) sugar syrup (page 7)
- 1 leaf titanium-strength gelatine, cut into quarters

FRANGELICO JELLY
- ⅔ cup (160 ml/5½ fl oz) Frangelico
- 2 tablespoons (40 ml/1½ fl oz) sugar syrup (page 7)
- 2 leaves titanium-strength gelatine, cut into quarters

CANDIED LIME GARNISH
- ½ cup (110 g/4 oz) sugar
- 1 lime, thinly sliced into rounds
- 1 tablespoon (15 g/½ oz) caster sugar

MOULD
any – total capacity of 1¾ cups
(430 ml/14½ fl oz)

1   Combine the liquid ingredients for each of the jellies in separate medium-sized heatproof bowls. Add 2 tablespoons (40 ml/1½ fl oz) water to the lime mixture and 3 tablespoons (60 ml/2 fl oz) water to the Frangelico mixture. Add the gelatine to each of the bowls and set aside for 5–10 minutes, until the gelatine has softened.

2   Set each bowl over a saucepan of simmering water and heat gently, stirring occasionally, until the gelatine dissolves.

3   Strain the liquids separately through a muslin-lined sieve (rinse the cloth between each batch). Cover the Frangelico mixture and keep at room temperature until required.

4   Pour the lime mixture into the mould and refrigerate for 15 minutes, or until semi set.

5   Add the Frangelico mixture, pouring slowly over the back of a dessert spoon resting against the inside of the mould. Refrigerate for 2–3 hours, until firm set.

6   Meanwhile, to make the candied lime garnish, combine the sugar with 3 table-spoons (60 ml/2 fl oz) water in a small saucepan. Bring to the simmer over low heat, stirring occasionally, until the sugar has dissolved. Add the lime slices to the sugar syrup. Simmer gently for 5 minutes, or until softened. Remove from the heat and set aside for 5 minutes.

7 Line a small tray with baking paper. Remove the lime slices using a fork, allowing them to drain slightly and arrange them onto the prepared tray. Set aside for 30–45 minutes, until the syrup begins to set thick and sticky.

8 Place the caster sugar in a small bowl. Cut the limes into small wedges, add them to the sugar and toss to coat. Transfer to a plate and set aside.

9 Unmould and top with the candied lime wedges to serve.

SERVES 4–6

You can serve this jelly in shot glasses instead of unmoulded. Set with slightly less gelatine (refer to conversion chart on page 5) and reverse the order of the jellies so that the lime layer is on top.

Piña Colada

- glacé cherries, to decorate

PINEAPPLE JELLY

- 1 large ripe pineapple, peeled,
  cored and coarsely chopped
- ⅓ cup (75 g/2½ oz) sugar
- ⅓ cup (80 ml/3 fl oz) white rum
- 3 leaves titanium-strength gelatine,
  cut into quarters

COCONUT JELLY

- ⅔ cup (160 ml/5½ fl oz) coconut milk
- 3 tablespoons (60 ml/2 fl oz) sugar syrup
  (page 7)
- 1½ tablespoons (30 ml/1 fl oz) white rum
- 1½ leaves titanium-strength gelatine,
  cut into quarters

MOULD
any – total capacity of 3 cups (750 ml/25 fl oz)

1   To prepare the pineapple jelly, combine the pineapple and sugar with 1 cup (250 ml/8½ fl oz) water in a medium saucepan. Bring to the boil over medium–high heat, then decrease the heat, cover and simmer for 30 minutes, or until the pineapple has softened. Mash the pineapple, using a potato masher and cook for 15 minutes, until softened and cooked through.

2   Spoon the mashed pineapple into a muslin-lined sieve and set aside to strain for about 15 minutes.

3   Pour the strained pineapple juice into a measuring jug (there should be around 1¼ cups/310 ml/10½ fl oz of liquid). Add the rum and enough water to make 2 cups (500 ml/17 fl oz) in total. Set aside to cool. Reserve 1 cup of the pineapple pulp, to decorate.

4   Meanwhile, to prepare the coconut jelly, combine the coconut milk, sugar syrup and rum in a bowl.

5   Place the gelatine for both jellies in separate medium-sized heatproof bowls and pour in just enough of the liquids to cover. Set aside for 5–10 minutes, until the gelatine has softened.

6   Set each bowl over a saucepan of simmering water and heat gently, stirring occasionally, until the gelatine dissolves. Remove from the heat, add the remainder of each liquid and stir to combine.

CONTINUED

7   Strain the liquids separately through a muslin-lined sieve (rinse the cloth between each batch). Cover the coconut mixture and keep at room temperature until required.

8   Arrange the cherries in the base of the mould and arrange some of the reserved pineapple pulp around them. Pour in enough pineapple mixture to just cover, and skim off any bubbles. Refrigerate for 10–30 minutes, until semi set.

9   Add the remaining pineapple mixture, pouring slowly over the back of a dessert spoon resting against the inside of the mould. Refrigerate for 20–60 minutes, until semi set.

10   Add the coconut mixture, pouring over the back of a spoon as before, and refrigerate for 2–4 hours, until firm set.

11   Unmould to serve.

SERVES 6

Tequila Sunrise Shots

ORANGE AND TEQUILA JELLY
- ¾ cup (180 ml/6 fl oz) orange juice
- 3 tablespoons (60 ml/2 fl oz) tequila
- 3 tablespoons (60 ml/2 fl oz) sugar syrup (page 7)
- 2 leaves gold-strength gelatine, cut into quarters

GRENADINE JELLY
- 1½ tablespoons (30 ml/1 fl oz) grenadine syrup
- ½ leaf gold-strength gelatine, cut into quarters

MOULD
4 x 80 ml (3 fl oz) shot glasses

This jelly can also be served unmoulded, as pictured. Make the mixture with a little more gelatine (refer to conversion chart on page 5) and, if you like, reverse the order of the layers. Refrigerate for 2–2½ hours, until firm set.

1   Pour the liquid ingredients for each of the jellies into separate medium-sized heatproof bowls. Add 2 tablespoons (40 ml/1½ fl oz) water to the grenadine. Add the gelatine to each of the bowls and set aside for 5–10 minutes, until the gelatine has softened.

2   Set each bowl over a saucepan of simmering water and heat gently, stirring occasionally, until the gelatine dissolves.

3   Strain the liquids separately through a muslin-lined sieve (rinse the cloth between each batch). Cover the orange and tequila mixture and keep at room temperature until required.

4   Divide the grenadine mixture evenly between the shot glasses and refrigerate for 5–10 minutes, until the mixture begins to thicken, but hasn't quite set.

5   Slowly pour two teaspoons of the orange and tequila mixture into the centre of each glass – it should blend slightly with the grenadine, to create a 'sunrise' effect. Refrigerate for 5–10 minutes, until semi set.

6   Divide the remaining orange and tequila mixture between the glasses and refrigerate for 1–1½ hours, until soft set.

SERVES 4

Bitter & Twisted

- 1 lemon
- 3¼ leaves titanium-strength gelatine, cut into quarters
- 1½ cups (375 ml/12½ fl oz) Indian tonic water
- ½ cup (110 g/4 oz) sugar
- ⅓ cup (80 ml/3 fl oz) gin
- 4–6 dashes Angostura bitters, to taste

MOULD
any – total capacity of 2 cups (500 ml/17 fl oz)

1   Use a small sharp knife to cut four thin rounds from the centre of the lemon. Cut the zest away from the flesh to make a long strip. Take both ends in your fingers and tightly twist and release, to create a lemon twist.

2   Place the gelatine into a medium-sized heatproof bowl and cover with ½ cup (125 ml/4 fl oz) of the tonic water. Set aside for 5–10 minutes, until the gelatine has softened.

3   Combine the sugar with ¾ cup (180 ml/6 fl oz) water in a small saucepan and heat gently over low heat, stirring occasionally, until the sugar dissolves. Add the lemon twists and simmer gently for 10 minutes, or until the liquid reduces by half and the lemon pith turns transparent. Remove the lemon zest, re-twist and set aside. Remove the sugar syrup from the heat, add the gelatine and tonic water mixture and stir until dissolved. Add the remaining tonic water, and the gin and bitters. Strain through a muslin-lined sieve.

4   Pour the mixture into the mould and refrigerate for 1 hour, or until the liquid begins to thicken and set slightly.

5   Remove from the refrigerator and lower the lemon twists into the jelly (they should suspend). Refrigerate for 3–4 hours, until firm set.

SERVES 4

For an extra 'twisted' effect, serve this jelly under a black light – it glows in the dark!

Glossary

Advocaat – a thick, sweet, Dutch liqueur made with egg yolks, sugar, brandy and vanilla. Available from liquor stores.

Blancmange – jelly made with milk instead of water.

Elderflower cordial – a highly aromatic cordial made from a thick sugar syrup infused with elderflowers. Available from gourmet food supply stores and some supermarkets.

Frangelico – a sweet hazelnut liqueur from Northern Italy. Available from liquor stores.

Lemon Verbena – a herb with long, tapered, fiborous, lemon-scented leaves which are used to infuse teas and desserts.

Matcha – a finely ground, high-grade Japanese green-tea powder, used to colour and flavour ice-cream and other Japanese sweets. Available from Asian grocers.

Moscato – a sweet, white, Italian dessert wine. Available from liquor stores.

Muslin cloth – a tightly-woven cotton fabric, available from speciality food supply stores and fabric shops.

Orange-blossom water – a fragrant, floral, orange-flavoured water, made from distilled orange blossoms. Available from some supermarkets, and Middle Eastern and gourmet food supply stores.

Prosecco – a dry Italian sparkling wine. Available from liquor stores.

Rosewater – a fragrant rose-flavoured water, made from distilled roses. Available from some supermarkets, and Middle Eastern and gourmet food supply stores.

Saffron threads – bright red threads, which are the handpicked stigmas from the saffron crocus. Saffron imparts a subtle, earthy, slightly bitter taste and a bright yellow colour when added to dishes. It is the world's most expensive spice and is used in small quantities in Middle Eastern and Mediterranean cuisine. Available from supermarkets and gourmet food supply stores.

Black sambuca – a sweet Italian aniseed-flavoured liqueur, with a deep blue–black colour. Available from liquor stores.

Violet Syrup – a sweet French syrup made from a thick sugar syrup infused with violet flower extract. Used to flavour desserts, as well as drinks and cocktails. Available from speciality gourmet food supply stores.

Index

PENGUIN BOOKS

Published by the Penguin Group
Penguin Group (Australia)
250 Camberwell Road, Camberwell, Victoria 3124, Australia
(a division of Pearson Australia Group Pty Ltd)

Penguin Books Ltd, Registered Offices: 80 Strand, London, WC2R 0RL, England

First published by Penguin Group (Australia), 2011

1 3 5 7 9 10 8 6 4 2

Text and photographs copyright © Penguin Group (Australia), 2011

Cover and text design by Marley Flory © Penguin Group (Australia)
Photography by Julie Renouf
Food preparation by Richenda Pritchard
Typeset in Gotham Narrow
Colour reproduction by Splitting Image P/L, Clayton, Victoria
Printed and bound in China by 1010 Printing International Limited

Cataloguing-in-Publication data is available from
the National Library of Australia

ISBN: 9780143565932

penguin.com.au